INSIDE CATHOLICISM

INRI

Grateful acknowledgment is made to the following for permission to reprint previously published material. Excerpt from *The Seven Storey Mountain* by Thomas Merton, copyright 1948 by Harcourt, Brace & Company and renewed 1976 by the Trustees of the Merton Legacy Trust, reprinted by permission of the publisher. Figure from *The Divine Comedy 1: Hell,* by Dante, translated by Dorothy L. Sayers, Penguin Classics, 1949, copyright C.W. Scott-Giles, 1949. Excerpt from *Early Christian Writings: The Apostolic Fathers,* translated by Maxwell Staniforth, Penguin Classics, 1968, copyright Maxwell Staniforth, 1968, reprinted by permission of the publisher. *Theological Investigations*, vol. 14, by Karl Rahner, copyright 1976 by Darton Longman & Todd Ltd., reprinted by permission of the publisher.

First published in USA 1995 by Collins Publishers San Francisco
Copyright ©1995 Collins Publishers San Francisco
Library of Congress Cataloging-in-Publication Data

McBrien, Richard P.
Inside Catholicism : rituals and symbols revealed / text by
Richard P. McBrien : edited by Barbara Roether.
 p. cm.
ISBN 0-00-649052-2
1. Catholic Church—Liturgy. 2. Sacraments—Catholic Church.
3. Sacraments (Liturgy) 4. Mass—Celebration. 5. Catholic Church—
Customs and practices. I. Roether, Barbara. II. Title.
BX1970.M395 1995
264'. 02—dc20   95-16468

Printed in China.

Inside Catholicism was designed and produced by Books Unbound
Signs of the Sacred series design concept by Tom Bonauro and John Choe
Text by Richard P. McBrien with additional caption material by Books Unbound

10 9 8 7 6 5 4 3 2 1

INSIDE CATHOLICISM

RITUALS AND SYMBOLS REVEALED

TEXT BY RICHARD P. McBRIEN

EDITED BY BARBARA ROETHER

CollinsPublishersSanFrancisco
A Division of HarperCollinsPublishers

TABLE OF CONTENTS

INTRODUCTION

The vast, multifaceted, and richly complex reality of Catholicism cannot easily be encompassed in a single volume. Catholicism is at once an international community of some one billion members; a historic tradition of some 2,000 years' duration; a way of life built upon such virtues as faith, hope, love, justice, and forgiveness; a highly intricate, hierarchically structured religious organization; and a vivid and aesthetically engaging composite of sacred rites known as sacraments and of other ritual practices. *Inside Catholicism* focuses particularly on this last aspect: the seven sacraments and the Church's other rituals of worship and devotion.

There are three overarching themes that define the total Catholic reality: the use of tangible signs of the invisible presence, or grace, of God; the sense of God's invisible presence working in people's lives through these visible signs, including other persons as well as rituals; and the sense of a communal relationship with the Church, and through the Church with God. In the language of contemporary Catholic theology, these three themes, or principles, are known as sacramentality, mediation, and communion.

Sacramentality: Visible Signs of Grace. Catholicism is essentially a religion of ritual signs and symbols through which we encounter the realm of the divine and the spiritual. There are seven such ritual signs with which Catholicism is historically identified. They are called the sacraments: Baptism, Confirmation, Eucharist (the Mass), Marriage, Holy Orders (including the priesthood, the episcopate, and the diaconate), Reconciliation (Penance, or Confession), and Anointing of the Sick (formerly known as Extreme Unction).

Many older Catholics will readily recall the familiar definition of a sacrament they learned from their catechism: "an outward sign instituted by Christ to give grace." Another definition offered more than 1,500 years ago by the great St. Augustine of Hippo may be less familiar, but it is even simpler: "a visible sign of an invisible grace." In 1963 Pope Paul VI provided a third, more contemporary, definition, which he applied directly to the Church: "a reality imbued with the hidden presence of God." Each definition points to the same fundamental truth: through the sacraments, humanity touches and is touched by the presence of God. The Church's seven sacraments, therefore, can only be understood within the larger context of the principle of sacramentality itself.

Simply put, the principle of sacramentality means that there is more to human life and cosmic reality than meets the eye. There is a "beyond" in our midst. There is a deeper, unseen reality—Being itself—that is in fact more "real" than all the beings that we take to be real. A sacramental perspective, therefore, is one that "sees" Being in beings, the divine in the human, the infinite in the finite, the spiritual in the material, the supernatural in the natural, the holy in the secular, the eternal in the temporal. For Catholicism all reality is sacred, or sacramental, because all reality is but a visible expression of invisible Reality itself, which is God.

In addition to the seven sacraments there are also a countless number of sacramentals, that is, devotional rituals and sacred objects that are similar to sacraments but that do not offer the same divine assurances of grace. Unlike the sacraments, sacramentals do not cause grace by the inherent power of Jesus Christ. Sacramentals cause grace in proportion to the faith and devotion of those who receive or use them. The sacramentals include: holy water; the ashes distributed on Ash Wednesday; the crucifix; the palms distributed on Palm Sunday; a blessed medal worn around the neck; a pair of rosary beads; a statue of Jesus, the Blessed Mother, or a saint; the blessing of an automobile, an animal, or a prayer book; Benediction of the Blessed Sacrament; and the stations of the cross.

As expressed in its sacraments and sacramentals, therefore, the Catholic vision "sees" God in all things: people, events, places, objects, nature, the whole cosmos, even in the passage of time itself (feast days, liturgical seasons). The visible, the tangible, the finite, the historical—all these are actual or potential bearers of the divine presence. For the Catholic it is only in and through these material realities that one can encounter the invisible God.

Employing a wider sense of the term *sacrament,* Jesus Christ is the great sacrament of our encounter with God. He is the fullest and most vivid expression, or sign, of God's presence in the world, and also the fullest and most vivid expression, or sign, of humanity's response to the divine presence. Because God is totally spiritual while human beings are material as well as spiritual, the humanity of Jesus becomes the bridge by which God and the human community meet. The Church, in turn, is the sacrament of encounter with Christ. It is the Body of Christ, the communal sign of Christ's abiding presence in history, bringing God to humanity and humanity to God. And the seven sacraments are the signs and instruments by which the encounter with Christ in the Church is ritually expressed and celebrated.

Of all the sacraments, the Eucharist (the central act of Catholic worship, known also as the Mass), is the most important. According to the Second Vatican Council, the Eucharist is "the summit toward which the activity of the Church is directed; at the same time it is the fountain from which all its power flows."

The abiding fear or concern of non-Catholic Christians, particularly Protestants, is that Catholics may carry the principle of sacramentality too far. Instead of maintaining the distinction between the visible sign and that which is signified (the divine reality itself), Catholics may collapse the two so that the sign takes on a kind of divine aura in itself. A statue of the Blessed Virgin Mary, for example, is no longer simply a means of raising the mind and heart to God; it becomes itself an object of worship. What Protestants fear most about the principle of sacramentality is the ever-present temptation to idolatry, that is, of confusing the human with the divine and of according the human what only the divine is worthy of receiving, namely, adoration.

Mediation: Means of Grace. In Catholic teaching a sacrament not only visibly signifies the invisible, active presence of God, which is also called grace; a sacrament actually causes what it signifies. The word *grace* means "gift" or "favor." The "gift" is God, and the "favor" is eternal life. Sacraments both signify and communicate this "gift" or "favor" known as grace. God is not only present as an object of faith in a sacrament; God actually achieves a spiritual effect in and through the sacrament. A sacrament, therefore, is both a sign and a cause of grace. In fact, the grace of a sacrament is always given unless the recipient is in the state of mortal sin, that is, of total alienation from God.

As causes of grace, sacraments mediate between God and humanity. A sacrament brings God to people, and people to God. God acts in the sacraments to communicate divine life, or grace; people act in the sacraments to express their adoration, thanksgiving, sorrow for sin, and their needs and hopes.

Catholicism's commitment to, and practice of, the principle of mediation is evident especially in the central role it accords the Church in carrying out Christ's work of redemption and salvation, and in the particular role it accords the priest in the life and rituals of the Church. Priests continue the work of Christ, the Mediator, by making the sacraments available to the whole community. At the Eucharist, in particular, the priest who presides over or celebrates the sacrament brings God's self-gift to the worshiping community in the preached word and in the consecrated bread and wine (Holy Communion). The priest also offers the community's own gifts to God, namely, all the personal sacrifices on behalf of others that are incorporated and expressed in the bread and wine that were brought to the altar.

However, it is not only the priest but the whole Church, including the laity, that mediates the presence and grace of God. "For their part," the Second Vatican Council declared, "the faithful join in the offering of the Eucharist by virtue of their royal priesthood."

The presence of God, however, can be mediated in many different ways, apart from the formal rituals of the Church. One of these ways is through mystical experience, that is, through some personally vivid experience of the presence of God. Christian mysticism is rooted in the baptismal call of all members of the Church to enter into the divine mystery through exposure and response to the presence of God in Sacred Scripture, the Eucharist, and the other sacraments. It is neither the product of special individual effort, nor is it a gift reserved for the spiritually elite. According to some of the early Christian writers, such as the anonymous sixth-century author known as Denys the Areopagite, whose works had a profound influence on medieval mystical theology, mysticism can be a dimension of every Christian's life.

Not all mystics, therefore, experience ecstasy, visions, or other altered states. In fact, none of these is a necessary indicator of mystical experience. Mysticism is essentially a process or way of life rather than a series of isolated and unusual experiences. The word that true mystics most frequently use to describe the heart of Christian mysticism is *union*. Indeed, it was the deep union of medieval saints like Bernard of Clairvaux, Francis of Assisi, and Catherine of Siena, and later of post-Reformation saints like Ignatius of Loyola, that led them into greater activity and service to others. Through the "mediation" of their own mystical experience of God, they became, in turn, effective "mediators" of the presence of God for others.

Communion: With God and with Others. Catholicism also affirms the principle of communion, or community. This means that humanity's way to God and God's way to humanity is not only a mediated way, but also a communal way. We are a people fractured by sin, which is a deliberate falling below God's moral standards for human living, as well as other forms of human weakness, but we are destined for reconciliation and healing at history's end. Even when the divine-human encounter is most personal and individual (as in private prayer, meditation, or even mystical experience), the encounter of God and humanity remains always communal because it is made possible by the mediation of a community of faith, the Church. In Catholicism there is no relationship with God, however personally profound or intense, that can dispense entirely with the communal context of every relationship with God. And just as the communal is the necessary context and condition for humanity's encounter with God and for God's encounter with humanity, so the realization of community is also the objective and the goal of the divine-human encounter itself.

The ultimate purpose of Christianity in general and of Catholicism in particular is the union of God and humanity. The promise and the hope that are at the root of Catholic and Christian faith are the promise and the hope of eternal life, of life in communion with God and with one another in God. Everything the Church does—its preaching and teaching, its moral behavior and discipline, its sacraments and rituals—is directed toward the fulfillment of the redemptive work of Jesus Christ himself, which is literally a work of atonement, or at-one-ment. All is for the sake of unity. All is for the sake of comm-unity.

Nowhere is this fundamental religious commitment to, and experience of, community more vividly expressed than in the sacramental life of the Church. Baptism initiates new members into the community of faith on earth and makes them heirs of the eternal community in heaven, an eternal state of being beyond human history where the union with God and with one another begun here on earth reaches its final and perfect fulfillment. Confirmation ratifies and strengthens the bonds of communion with the Church, both on earth and in heaven. The Eucharist is the highest expression of the union that the various members of the Church, the Body of Christ, have with one another, in Christ and with Christ through the power of the Holy Spirit, and it is also the ritual anticipation of the community we are destined to enjoy around the heavenly banquet table. It is important to note that heaven, the final state of happiness where the righteous, or "the pure of heart" (Matthew 5:8), are united forever with God and with all of the other righteous, was depicted by Jesus in terms of feasting at a wedding banquet (Matthew 22:1–14). Marriage creates a new union between a woman and a man and looks toward the building, upon that union, of a new community we call the family. Holy Orders initiates one into a community of priests and deacons united with their bishop—a union of ordained ministers in the service of the faith-community, the local church or diocese. The sacrament of Reconciliation, or Penance, restores a sinner's union with the wider faith-community, a union broken by serious sin. Anointing of the Sick restores a sick or dying member to that faith-community, brings the prayers and concerns of the community to those who are seriously ill, and prepares one for entrance into the heavenly community.

The way in which these sacraments are celebrated, however, is not absolutely uniform within the Catholic Church. Though standard in content, rituals may be expressed in slightly different ways, even within the same city. Some churches will adapt ritual language and forms to meet the particular needs of the parish. Contrary to a widespread popular perception, the Catholic Church is, in fact, a plurality of churches differentiated by a diversity of sacred rituals that pertain to worship. It is a communion of churches, united with one another and with the Bishop of Rome (the pope). The *Roman* Catholic Church is the largest, but not the only, church within the family of Catholic churches. There are seven other non-Latin, non-Roman, Oriental ritual traditions within the Catholic Church: Armenian, Byzantine, Coptic, Ethiopian, East Syrian (Chaldean), West Syrian, and Maronite. Each of these Eastern-rite churches is a Catholic church in the fullest sense of the word. Catholicism, therefore, is neither narrowly Roman nor narrowly Western. It is universal, which is what the adjective *Catholic* means.

In an ecumenical age such as our own, major Protestant theologians have come to an increasingly sympathetic appreciation of the Catholic principles of sacramentality, mediation, and communion—just as Catholic theologians have come to a deeper understanding of and respect for Protestantism's historic concerns about Catholicism. Thus, for Langdon Gilkey, a distinguished Baptist theologian who taught for many years in the Divinity School at the University of Chicago, Catholicism manifests "a remarkable sense of humanity and grace in the communal life of Catholics. . . . Consequently the love of life, the appreciation of the body in the senses, of joy and celebration, the tolerance of the sinner—these natural, worldly, and 'human' virtues are far more clearly and universally embodied in Catholics and Catholic life than in Protestants and Protestantism." Indeed, Professor Gilkey concludes, Catholicism's principle of sacramentality "may provide the best entrance into a new synthesis of the Christian tradition with the vitalities as well as the relativities of contemporary existence" (*Catholicism Confronts Modernity: A Protestant View,* New York: Seabury Press, 1975, pp. 17–18, 20–22).

Inside Catholicism is a visually rich exposition that also provides an "entrance into . . . the vitalities as well as the relativities of contemporary [Catholic] existence." To be sure, there are many other possible entranceways, but Catholicism's sacraments and rituals offer us one of the most inviting and most accessible of all.

Richard P. McBrien

ENTERING
THE RITUAL SPACE

1

In the sacred spaces that the church occupies to preach the Word of God and celebrate the sacraments, especially the Eucharist, forming community is central. The altar as a symbol of Christ himself is the central focus of attention, situated where all can easily see it. It is, like Christ, a point of intersection between God and humanity, the place where he becomes present to the community in the sacrament of the Eucharist and where the community offers its own sacrifice of praise and thanksgiving to God, in union with Christ's sacrifice on the cross. The placement within the sanctuary of the baptismal font and the lectern (pulpit), and the placement of the pews, often in a fan shape around the altar and sanctuary, all underscore the purpose of the sacred space, which is communal worship.

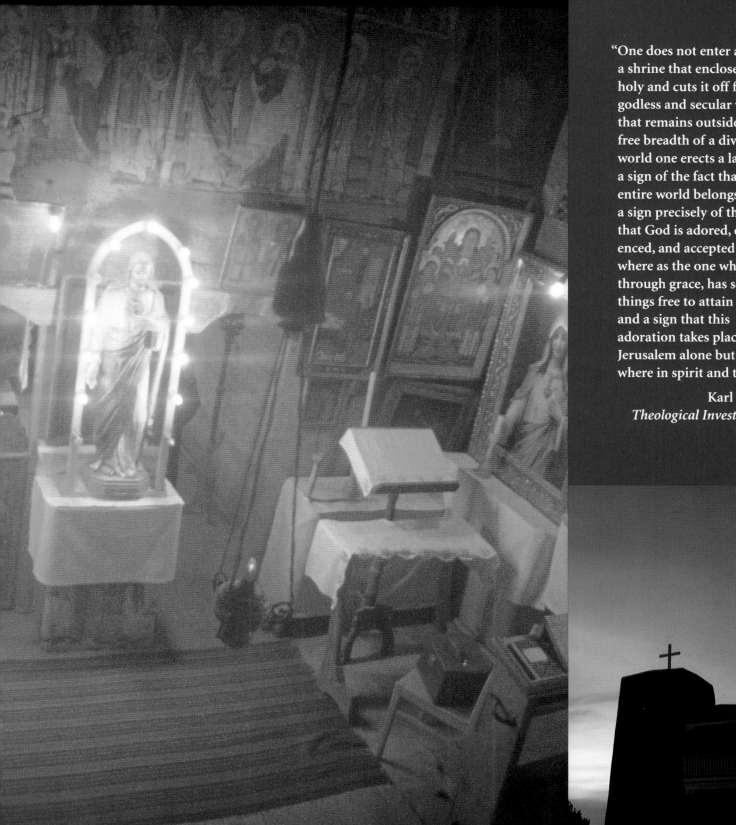

"One does not enter a temple, a shrine that encloses the holy and cuts it off from a godless and secular world that remains outside. In the free breadth of a divine world one erects a landmark, a sign of the fact that this entire world belongs to God, a sign precisely of the fact that God is adored, experienced, and accepted everywhere as the one who, through grace, has set all things free to attain to him, and a sign that this adoration takes place not in Jerusalem alone but everywhere in spirit and truth."

Karl Rahner,
Theological Investigations

A complete organizational chart of the Catholic Church would easily fill a whole page, and would not be easy to draw. Most people expect the pope to appear at the top of an imagined hierarchy as the chief executive officer. However, an ecumenical council also possesses supreme authority in the Church. Below the pope is situated a highly bureaucratized Roman Curia composed of congregations, cardinals, archbishops, bishops, monsignors, priests, and lay assistants, along with the College of Cardinals (1), which has a direct advisory relationship to the pope and which elects a new pope. There is the Synod of Bishops (2), which is drawn from hierarchies throughout the entire Catholic world and meets every few years. Under these international bodies are various national conferences of bishops, bishops of individual dioceses, and other levels of intermediate authority, all the way down to parish priests (3) and lay ministers.

With Vatican Council II (1962–65), the Catholic Church moved away from the traditional pyramidal concept of authority to one of shared responsibility, rooted especially in the biblical image of the people of God. The Church, the council taught, is composed of many different kinds of members (laity, religious, and clergy alike), possessing many different kinds of gifts, or *charisms*, and fulfilling many different roles. The task of the hierarchy, the pope and bishops, is to help all the faithful, laity and clergy alike, to fulfill the mission which Jesus Christ gave to every baptized member of the Church. Today the organizational image of the Church might translate to a series of concentric circles all on the same level.

The pope celebrates a special Mass on the Papal Altar of St. Peter's Basilica in the Vatican. The altar, covered by Bernini's canopy, rises over the tomb of St. Peter, the first pope, who was martyred in Rome in AD 64. Since 1377, following nearly seventy years in residence at Avignon, France, the popes have resided in the Vatican, which serves as the temporal and spiritual center of the Catholic Church.

The Cross. The cross is the preeminent symbol of Christianity, calling to mind the Crucifixion and Resurrection of Christ. Physically, spatially, mentally, and spiritually, the cross informs the rituals of the Church. The pervasive symbol of the cross lends its shape to the floor plans of the Church's great cathedrals. At the intersection of the two aisles, near the imagined heart of Jesus Christ, the Mass is celebrated. Many variants of the cross are used, the Latin cross (A) being the most common. The Celtic cross, (B) and the Greek cross (C) are also used.

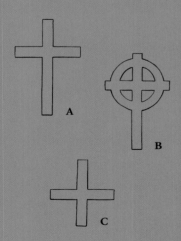

A

B

C

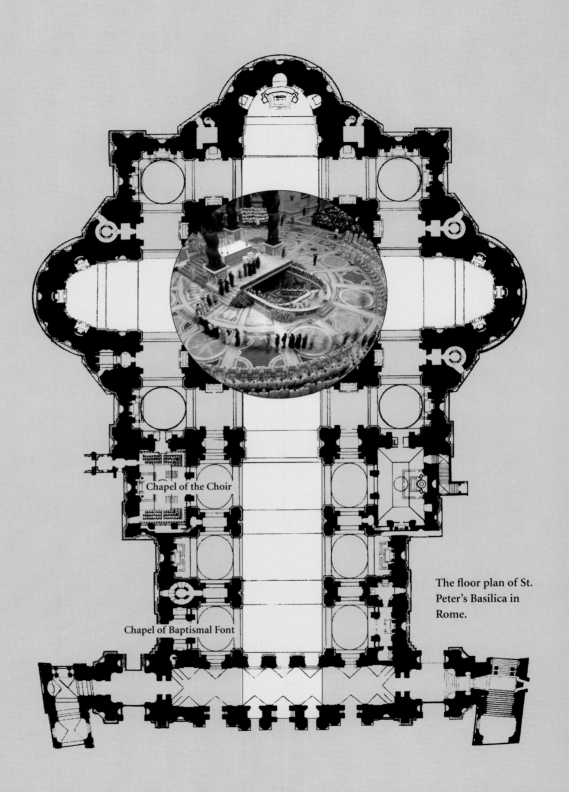

Chapel of the Choir

Chapel of Baptismal Font

The floor plan of St. Peter's Basilica in Rome.

St. Jerome, the Virgin Mary, St. John, and Mary Magdalene attend the death of Christ on the cross. St. Jerome (who was born in the fourth century) once threw himself in front of a crucifix to ward off the temptations of lust. He is followed by a lion from whose paw he once removed a thorn. The lion is thought of as the king of beasts, as Christ is King of the Jews. The bridge over the waters shows Christ's death as the bridge to immortality; the castle marks his heavenly kingdom. Mary Magdalene stands by a vase of oil she has brought to anoint Jesus for burial. The open gate behind her is a symbol of female chastity.

MARKING THE BODY WITH THE SIGN OF THE CROSS

1. In the name of the Father,

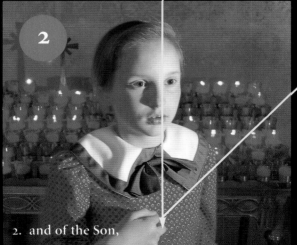

2. and of the Son,

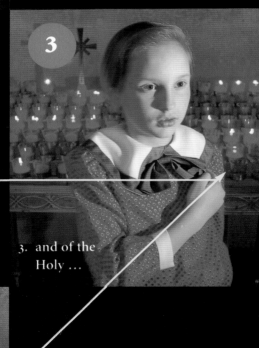

3. and of the Holy …

4. … Spirit. Amen.

24

TRIANGLE

TREFOIL

TRIQUETRA

THE HOLY TRINITY

Catholics believe that God is revealed through three Persons, who manifest different aspects of God and are one in God, coequal and coeternal. They are the Father, the Son, and the Holy Spirit or Holy Ghost. A number of symbols are used to represent the Holy Trinity. The Father is symbolized by the all-seeing eye and by the hand; the Son by the crucified Christ or a lamb; and the Holy Spirit by the dove.

The hand of God reaches out to touch the hand of man in this detail from Michelangelo's Sistine Chapel.

The symbols of the Trinity are apparent in the architectural details of Gothic cathedrals.

FATHER

SON

HOLY SPIRIT

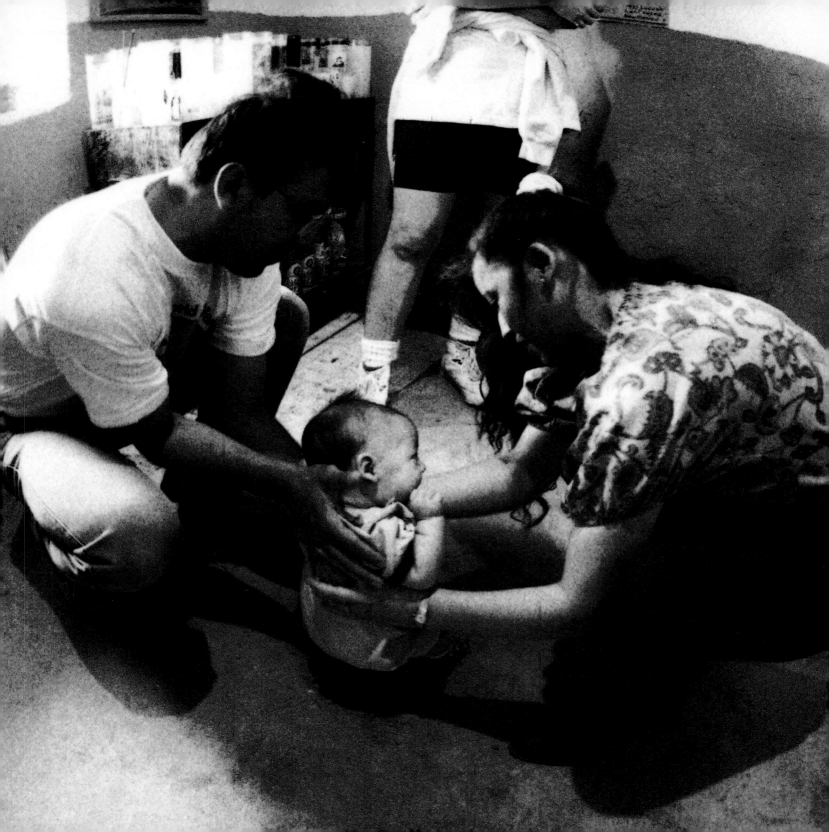

SACRAMENTS OF
INITIATION

2

SACRAMENTS OF INITIATION

The sacraments of initiation: Baptism, Confirmation and Eucharist (First Communion), bring the faithful to the full stature of Christ and enable them to carry out the mission of the Church within the faith-community and in the world at large. Through the waters of Baptism and the power of the Holy Spirit, the new members, young and mature alike, are incorporated into the Body of Christ, are formed into God's people, and receive forgiveness of their sins. In Confirmation they are signed with the gift of the Holy Spirit, become more perfectly the image of Christ, are empowered with the Spirit to bear witness before all the world, and to work for the building up of the Body of Christ. In the Eucharist, finally, they come to the table of the Lord, to be nourished by the Body and Blood of Christ so that they might have eternal life and reflect the unity of God's people.

The Apple. The Latin word *malum* can mean either apple or "evil," (as in malice). Through this play on words the forbidden fruit has come to be the symbol of forbidden knowledge. When Eve plucked the apple from the "tree of the knowledge of good and evil" in the garden of Eden, she sent humanity on the uncertain road out of ignorant bliss.

A traditional Catholic notion that Baptism washes away a moral stain, known as Original Sin (the sin of Adam and Eve), is no longer widely held in the Church. Current thinking views Original Sin as the condition into which all humans are born, that is, a world in which suffering, among other factors, circumscribes our freedom—an idea akin to Buddhist *samsara*, the inherent suffering in human existence. The difficulty of this human situation is compounded by a lack of spiritual energy or grace, a grace that is restored through the renewal of the sacrament of Baptism.

Water/The Baptismal Font. The use of water as a purifying substance is universal. Water is also symbolic of the oceanic beginnings of life, and human life which emerges from the amniotic waters of the womb. When the priest says, "Unseal for us the fountain of Baptism," he is referring to this ancient sense of the font, whose waters give birth to a newly born Christian.

Raphael painted Saint John the Baptist with the infant Jesus and Mary. The two were relatives and, according to legend, childhood playmates. John wears a camel hair cloak, a sign of the ascetic life he will lead in the desert. John is seen as a precursor to Jesus; he was a powerful teacher who baptized his many followers. When the two were grown John baptized Jesus in the river Jordan, and was quick to hail him as a messiah.

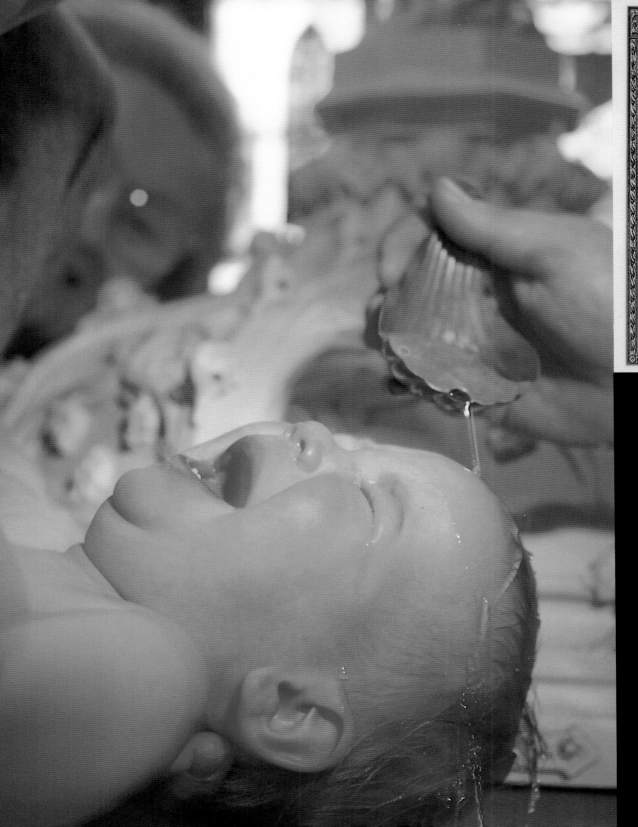

BAPTISM

"By water and the Holy Spirit, this child is to receive the gift of new life in faith from God Who is Love." As the priest pours water over the child three times, he recites the actual words of the baptism: "I baptize you in the name of the Father, and of the Son, and of the Holy Spirit. Amen."

At the beginning of this Baptism ritual, the priest marks the chest of the infant with oil while reciting the words he has adapted from the standard Baptism ritual, "We anoint you with the oil of salvation, the balm of Gilead, the costly oil of Bethany, in the name of Christ our Savior. May he strengthen you with his power. Amen."

The oil of chrism and the oil of catechumens are blessed at a special Chrism Mass, which is traditionally held on Holy Thursday. Oil of chrism, which is olive oil mixed and perfumed with other precious oils, is part of many Catholic rituals. The oil is intended to visibly mark the catechumens with the shining symbol of their faith. Chrism comes from the Greek *chrisma* and means "anointing." Christ's name means the Anointed One.

God of wonder and majesty, look now with love upon us and unseal for us the fountain of baptism. By the power of your Holy Spirit, give this water the grace of your Son, so that in this sacrament of Baptism all those who have been created in your likeness may be washed over by your love."

Someone from the family lights the child's candle from the Easter candle. The celebrant says, "Receive the light of Christ. Parents and godparents, this light is entrusted to you to keep burning brightly. This child of yours has been enlightened by Christ. He is to walk always as a child of the light."

The celebrant touches the ears and the mouth of the child with his thumb, and says, "The Lord Jesus made the deaf hear and the dumb speak. May ___ ___ he open to hear the Word of God, and your mouth open to proclaim our faith to the praise and glory of God."

Child, you have become a new creation, and have clothed yourself in Christ. See in this white garment the outward sign of your Christian dignity. With your family and friends to help you by word and example, live in that dignity which is yours by virtue of God's love for you."

Adult Baptism. Before Vatican II, infant baptism was generally regarded as the ordinary means of entrance into the Church. Adult baptism was the exception. In either case, Baptism was celebrated as an individual sacrament, unrelated to any other except as the precondition for receiving the other sacraments later in life. Calling for a return to ancient practices (when adult baptism was the norm), the Second Vatican Council encouraged the development of a new ritual, the Rite of Christian Initiation of Adults, known as RCIA. The ideal embodied in RCIA is that a person should receive the three sacraments of initiation together—Baptism, Confirmation, and Eucharist—during the annual celebration of the Easter Vigil and after a suitable period of formation known as the catechumate. Following this initiation, the new Christian continues to be instructed in the faith not only in word but also by the example of the local faith community of which he or she is now a part.

During the Lenten Season
Please pray for:

Nashia C. Raley
Catechumen

who will be Baptized, Confirmed and
receive First Eucharist
at the Easter Vigil
April 15, 1995

FIRST COMMUNION

Children receive First Communion soon after the age of reason (around seven years old), when they can clearly understand that the consecrated bread and wine of Communion are the Body and Blood of Christ. For generations of Catholic children, First Communion has been a memorable first encounter with the sacramental presence of Christ.

Remembrance of my
First Holy Communion

The theme of purification in preparation for the sacrament (fasting as purification of the body, confession of sin as purification of the conscience) is reflected in wearing clothing that is white—the color of purity and innocence. White is also the color of the baptismal garment. When Baptism, First Communion, and Confirmation were performed at the same time the same clothing was worn throughout.

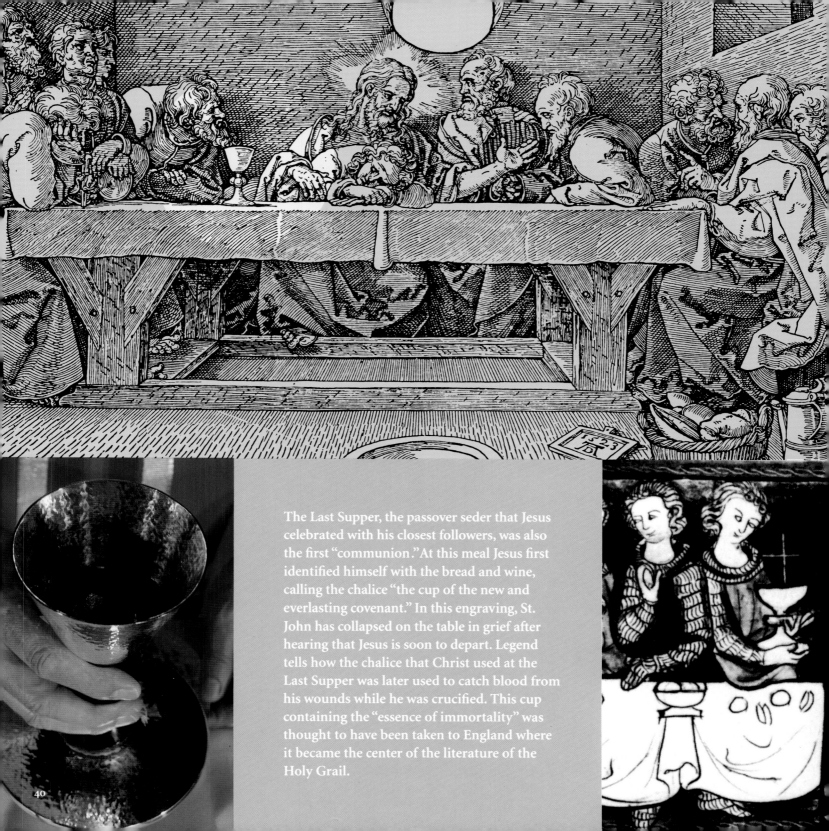

The Last Supper, the passover seder that Jesus celebrated with his closest followers, was also the first "communion." At this meal Jesus first identified himself with the bread and wine, calling the chalice "the cup of the new and everlasting covenant." In this engraving, St. John has collapsed on the table in grief after hearing that Jesus is soon to depart. Legend tells how the chalice that Christ used at the Last Supper was later used to catch blood from his wounds while he was crucified. This cup containing the "essence of immortality" was thought to have been taken to England where it became the center of the literature of the Holy Grail.

Overwhelmed by the grandeur of the occasion, a boy receives his First Communion but is unsure exactly what to do next. Generally, a joyous atmosphere prevails at First Communion. The children are delighted to finally participate in a ritual they have up to now witnessed from afar.

Confirmation. Though Church law holds that Confirmation should come after Baptism but before First Communion, many American dioceses confirm children after First Communion, in early adolescence. Confirmation then acts as a sort of coming of age ritual within the Church, and helps prepare the young person for adult life as a Catholic. The graduation gowns worn here support the sense of these students having graduated to full status as responsible members of the Church, who vow to lead lives that bear witness to Christ's presence as they move through the world.

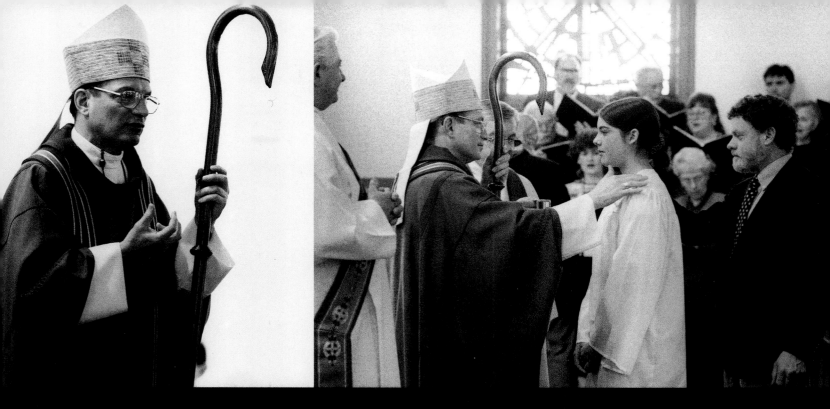

CONFIRMATION

THE MASS

③

The Mass, or Eucharist
(literally "thanksgiving"), was
first celebrated as a meal. The
original eucharistic meal was
the Last Supper, which Jesus
ate with his apostles the night
before he was crucified. At
this meal he identified himself with the bread and wine
they were sharing, and knowing that his own death was
imminent, instructed his followers to "do this in memory
of me." In the early Church
this tradition of shared meals
in Christ's memory was continued, and eventually developed into the more elaborate
rite we know today. The term
mass is derived from the
Latin word *missa,* which
means "dismissal," the closing
blessing at the Eucharist.
From the earliest years the
Eucharist was celebrated on
Sunday, as a commemoration
of the Resurrection. At the
center of the Mass is the
prayer of thanksgiving, once
called the Canon of the Mass
and now known as the
Eucharistic Prayer.

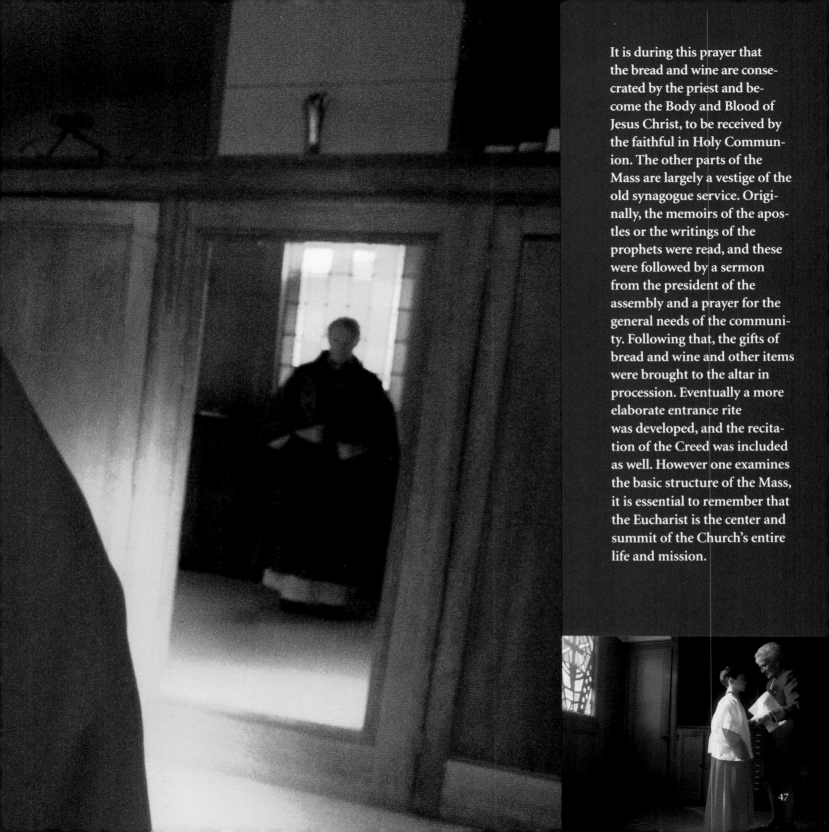

It is during this prayer that the bread and wine are consecrated by the priest and become the Body and Blood of Jesus Christ, to be received by the faithful in Holy Communion. The other parts of the Mass are largely a vestige of the old synagogue service. Originally, the memoirs of the apostles or the writings of the prophets were read, and these were followed by a sermon from the president of the assembly and a prayer for the general needs of the community. Following that, the gifts of bread and wine and other items were brought to the altar in procession. Eventually a more elaborate entrance rite was developed, and the recitation of the Creed was included as well. However one examines the basic structure of the Mass, it is essential to remember that the Eucharist is the center and summit of the Church's entire life and mission.

47

On entering church it is traditional to dip the hand in the font of holy water and make the sign of the cross over one's body. It is a symbolic cleansing that helps prepare one for the Mass by marking the passage from the secular world to the sacred, and actually washing one's hands and face was once the custom. After purifying themselves with holy water, Catholics genuflect in the aisle before

The Liturgy of the Word and the Liturgy of the Eucharist are the two main parts of every Mass. The Liturgy of the Word begins with a reading from the Old Testament and a prayer from the psalms, followed by a reading from the letters of St. Paul or the apostles, a reading from the Gospel, and a homily or sermon. The Liturgy of the Eucharist begins with the presentation of the gifts through the processional, and is followed by the Eucharistic Prayer, and finally, the celebration of Communion.

The gifts—unconsecrated communion hosts, water, wine, and money
from the collection—are carried from
the back of the church to the altar in
the processional. The processional
originated when bread and wine for
the Eucharist were carried by early
Christians from their homes and
brought to the priest to share at Mass.
Gifts of precious jewels, gold, or live-
stock were once common offerings for
the collection, and Gothic cathedrals
contained rooms to store the donated
wealth.

The priest mixes water into the wine while saying, "By the mystery of this water and wine may we come to share in the divinity of Christ, who humbled himself to share in our humanity." In Christ's time, wine was diluted with water before drinking, and this tradition has continued in the Eucharist. Having completed the initial preparation of the gifts, the priest washes his hands, saying, "Lord, wash away my iniquity; cleanse me from my sin."

The Sign of Peace. Christ said to his disciples, "I leave you peace, my peace I give you." Since every member of the Church is part of the "priesthood of believers," all can offer each other the peace of God. Some physical contact, as well as a spoken greeting of goodwill, is

Holding the host in his hands, the priest repeats the ancient formula that transforms the bread and wine into the Body and Blood of Christ. Taking up the bread he says, "Take this, all of you, and eat: This is my body which will be given up for you." Taking up the wine, he says, "Take this, all of you, and drink from it: This is the cup of my blood, the blood of the new and everlasting covenant. It will be shed for

Then raising both bread and wine which have now become the Body and Blood of Christ, the priest concludes the Eucharistic Prayer with a final praise, saying or singing, "Through him, with him, and in him, in the unity of the Holy Spirit, all glory and honor is yours

The priest continues to prepare the gifts for distribution. He breaks the consecrated host, thereby repeating the most ancient of Christian liturgical gestures—the breaking of bread. He then drops a piece of the host into the wine to symbolize the mingling of the Body and Blood of Christ. He takes the two largest pieces of the host in his hand and says to the congregation, "This is the Lamb of God, who takes away the sins of the World. Happy are those who are called to his supper." The priest consumes the bread and wine and then distributes Communion.

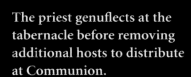

The priest genuflects at the tabernacle before removing additional hosts to distribute at Communion.

The chi rho symbol worn on the priest's chasuble consists of the first two letters of the Greek XPICTOC, which is pronounced Christos. This abbreviation of Christ's name has been in use for at least 1,600 years.

Consecrated by the priest through the ancient words of the Eucharistic Prayer, the bread and wine have become the Body and Blood of Christ. Those who partake of this communion with faith in the Real Presence of Christ become more deeply united with one another and with the Church, which is also the Body of Christ. The host is offered to each person with the words "Body of Christ." The receiver answers, "Amen," and takes the host either in the hand or directly onto the tongue. Once taken into the mouth, it may be chewed like ordinary food because it is indeed food for the spirit. The consecrated wine is offered separately to each person with the words "Blood of Christ." Even if not offered separately, the Blood of Christ is considered to be present in the host.

SACRAMENTS OF
VOCATION AND COMMITMENT

④

Two sacraments are directed immediately to one's life calling, or vocation—whether in married and family life (the sacrament of Marriage) or in the ministerial service of the Church (the sacrament of Holy Orders). Through the sacrament of Marriage, the Church is built up and manifested at its most natural, communal level. The sacrament celebrates and sanctifies the mutual love and commitment of two people who choose to bond themselves together in a covenant that is expressive of God's love for all humanity and of Christ's love for the Church. The family, which is the principal fruit of marriage, has been called the "domestic church." According to Pope John Paul II, "there should be found in every Christian family the various aspects of the entire Church."

MARRIAGE

A church wedding for this Catholic couple is more than a location of choice; by marrying in the Church, the couple commits themselves to the faith community. The marriage ritual includes the couple's affirmation of their freedom, their willingness to have children, and their commitment to bringing their children up in the Catholic Church.

Each Catholic marriage has two essential parts: the *ratum* is the rite at the church that binds the couple in commitment. It is the public sacramental aspect of the marriage. *Consummatum* seals the covenant with the physical act of union. The ring is a pre-Christian symbol of bonding and fidelity. Its use as a wedding band originates with the ancient Egyptians, who believed a love vein stretched from the heart to the fourth finger.

The metaphor of marriage, the joining of body and spirit, has also been applied to women who choose to join the sisterhood by becoming "Brides of Christ." Christ is also said to be "married" to his Church. From Teresa of Avila to Mother Teresa of Calcutta, the works of holy women in the Catholic Church are renowned. Although they live a life dedicated to the service of God, women cannot actually receive the sacrament of ordination. Their exclusion from this sacrament, and the prohibition against their leading the celebration of Mass, is one issue dividing the Catholic Church today.

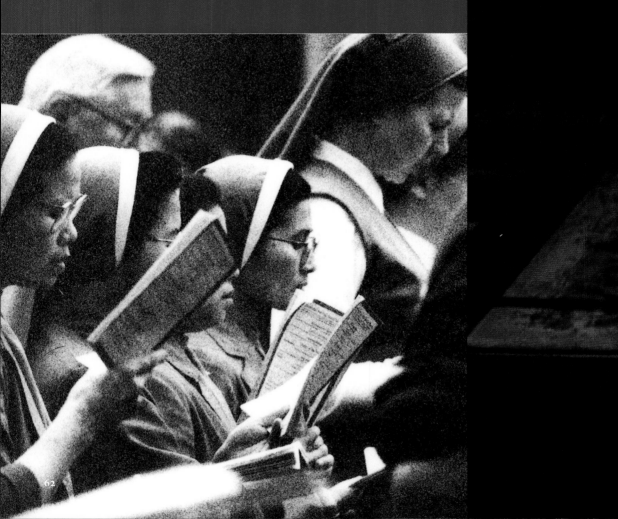

Holy Orders. The sacrament of Holy Orders is really three sacraments in one: diaconate, presbyterate, and episcopate; we know them as deacon, priest, and bishop. The deacon is ordained to provide direct ministerial assistance to the pastor or to the bishop. Historically, deacons were particularly responsible for care and outreach for the poor. Priests primarily provide religious care of a local community or parish. The bishop is ordained to provide the ministry of oversight (the literal meaning of the Greek word *episcopos,* from which the word *bishop* is derived) for a cluster of parishes known as a diocese. The act of women taking vows into the sisterhood is not considered a sacrament, though it is certainly a sacred covenant. The role of nuns in the community is as various as that of their male counterparts. They work as doctors, teachers, administrators, and as theologians and writers. Cloistered nuns and monks serve the community through the gift of prayer. Though the priesthood of Christ is conferred in a special way by ordination, the priesthood of Christ is shared by every baptized member of the Church, laity included.

HOLY ORDERS

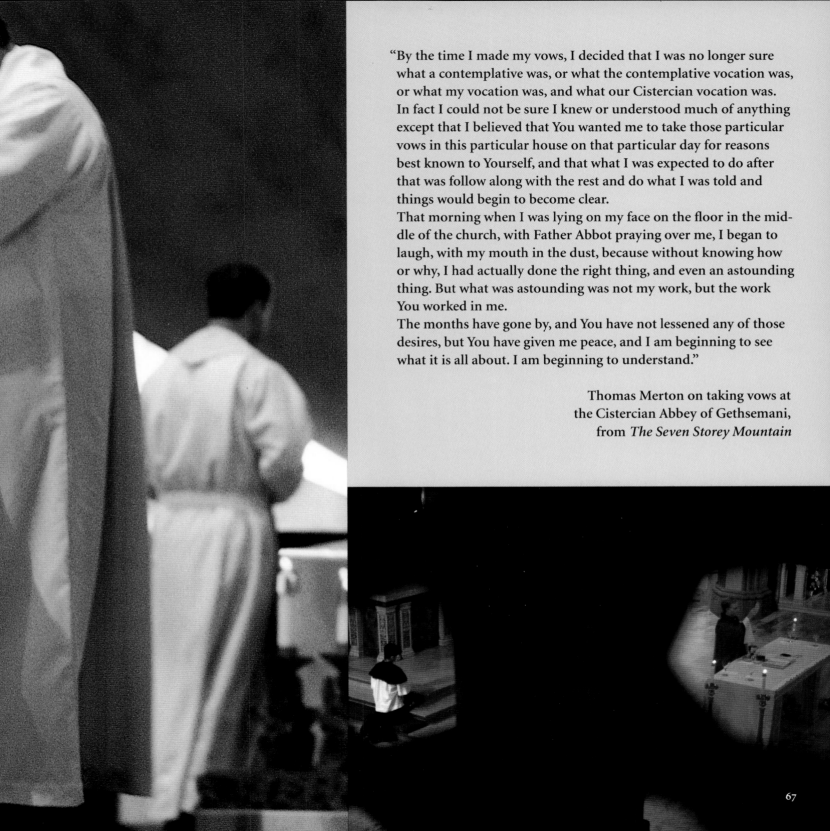

"By the time I made my vows, I decided that I was no longer sure what a contemplative was, or what the contemplative vocation was, or what my vocation was, and what our Cistercian vocation was. In fact I could not be sure I knew or understood much of anything except that I believed that You wanted me to take those particular vows in this particular house on that particular day for reasons best known to Yourself, and that what I was expected to do after that was follow along with the rest and do what I was told and things would begin to become clear.

That morning when I was lying on my face on the floor in the middle of the church, with Father Abbot praying over me, I began to laugh, with my mouth in the dust, because without knowing how or why, I had actually done the right thing, and even an astounding thing. But what was astounding was not my work, but the work You worked in me.

The months have gone by, and You have not lessened any of those desires, but You have given me peace, and I am beginning to see what it is all about. I am beginning to understand."

Thomas Merton on taking vows at
the Cistercian Abbey of Gethsemani,
from *The Seven Storey Mountain*

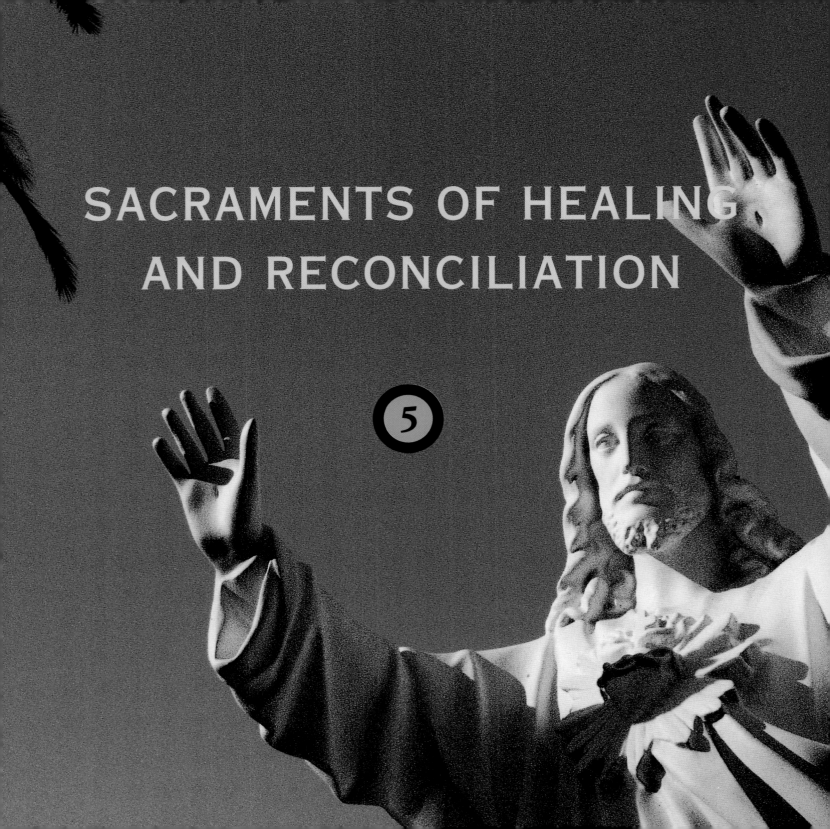

SACRAMENTS OF HEALING
AND RECONCILIATION

5

In almost every life, obstacles arise. Catholics believe such obstacles keep them from participating fully in the Christian life they have entered. Everyone, even members of the Church, is prone to sin and vulnerable to illness, physical weakness, and finally, death. Two sacraments are celebrated by the Church as signs and instruments of God's and of Christ's encompassing power to heal and forgive. The sacrament of Anointing of the Sick, formerly called Extreme Unction, is for those whose bond with the Church has been weakened by illness or other physical problems. This sacrament can be given to a group as well as an individual. The sacrament of Penance or Reconciliation, formerly known as Confession, is for those whose relationship to the Church has been strained or even severed by sin.

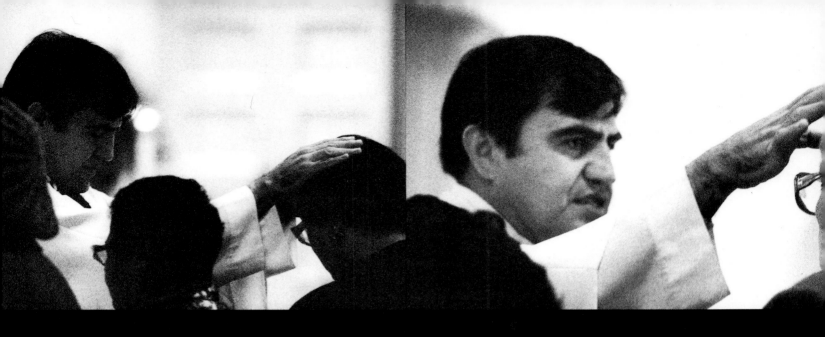

ANOINTING OF THE SICK

Priests anoint the sick of their parish in a special Mass. This anointing is not meant for those who are near death but for those who, by sickness or old age, might be in danger of dying. The number of anointings varies with the individual's situation; for terminally ill patients a personal anointing is offered each month. The ritual elements include a greeting, words to those present, a penitential rite (scripture, litany), the priest's laying on of hands, blessing of oil, prayer of thanksgiving, the anointing of the forehead and hands with oil.

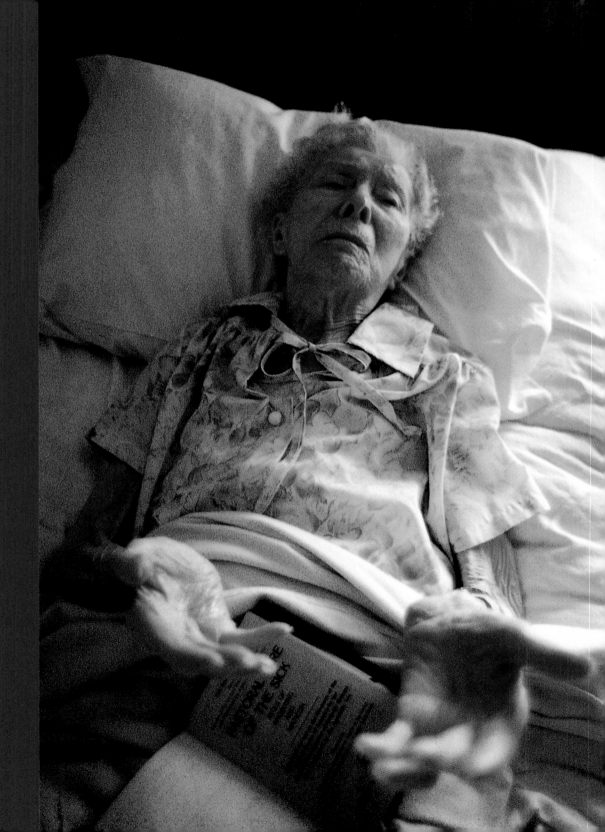

The purpose of both the sacrament of Anointing of the Sick and of Penance is to heal and to restore the physical and moral person so that he or she can once again enter into full communion with the Church. The Church is interested in healing and in the total health of the whole person and of the human community at large. The Church cannot abandon those who, by certain of the world's standards, are no longer of practical use, or whom society scorns or rejects: the drug addict, the victim of AIDS. In the sacrament of Penance the Church both forgives and is forgiven. The Church itself is also a penitent, bathing the feet of Christ with its tears and listening to his words from the cross: "Neither do I condemn you" (John 8:11). In the sacrament of Anointing, the Church reaches out to the sick and dying, energizing their faith and hope in Christ's promise of eternal life.

Extreme Unction, or Last Rites, is given to a
woman in a nursing home. The priest anoints
her hands and forehead with the healing oil of
chrism, and absolves her of any remaining sins.

Death has been swallowed up in victory.
Where, O Death, is your victory?
Where, O Death, is your sting?

1 Corinthians 15: 51–55

LAST RITES

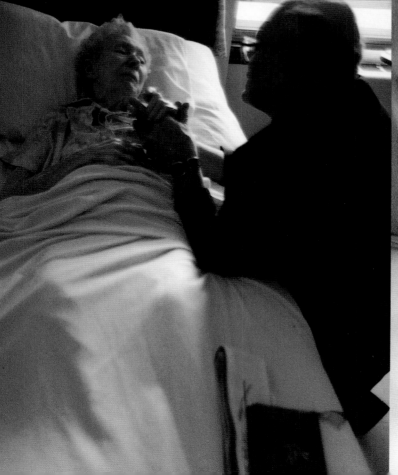

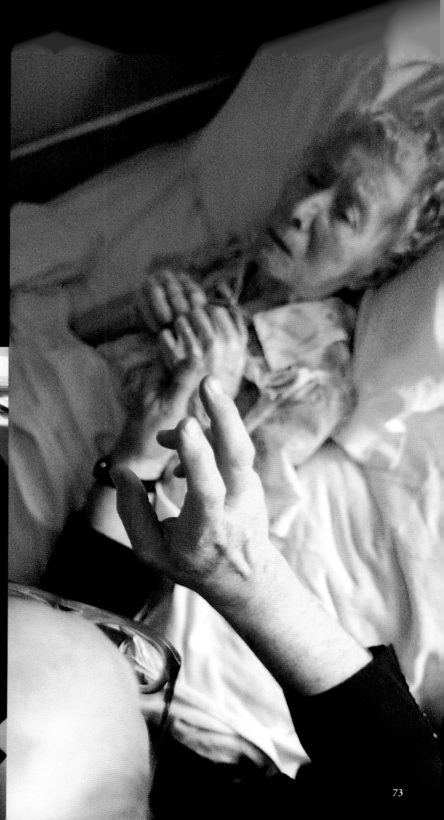

Milagros. Throughout the Americas and Mediterranean Europe, *milagros,* or "miracles," are used as a sacred currency to petition saints for healing or protection, and as a return gift for help already given. A silver breast might be given by a woman who has recovered from breast cancer, a heart by those with romantic wishes or those with heart disease. Animal figures are offered for the health of farm stock or for fertility. A golden arm is left by one whose broken arm has healed. Milagros are often seen pinned to wooden statues or left at the foot of a figure or shrine.

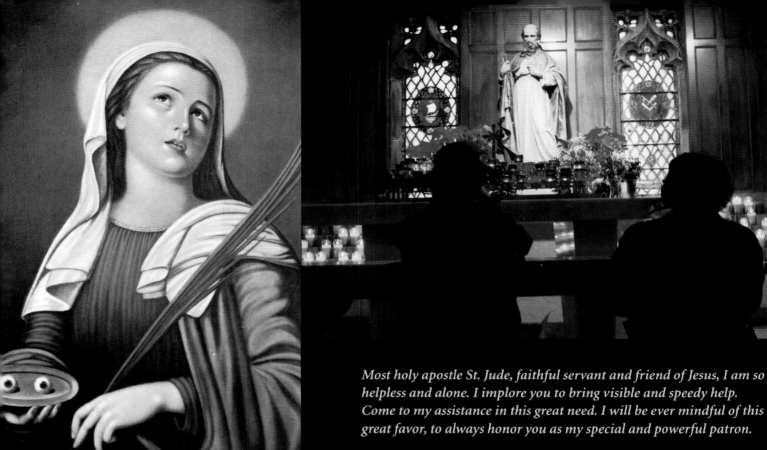

Most holy apostle St. Jude, faithful servant and friend of Jesus, I am so helpless and alone. I implore you to bring visible and speedy help. Come to my assistance in this great need. I will be ever mindful of this great favor, to always honor you as my special and powerful patron.

Among the congregation of saints are many with special associations for the sick or troubled. Among them is St. Lucy, who, according to legend, plucked out her own eyes and offered them to her fiancé when her family tried to prevent her from entering a convent. She is the saint invoked for those with vision problems or blindness. St. Jude Thaddeus, one of Jesus' apostles, is known as the patron saint of hopeless cases (such as shipwrecked sailors). A shrine to St. Jude in San Francisco attracts a steady stream of petitioners.

EYE MILAGRO

Reconciliation. In recent times the rite of Penance has been largely revised and is now referred to as Reconciliation. For generations of Catholics the opening words for the sacrament of Penance, "Bless me, Father, for I have sinned," represented the very essence of Catholic sorrow for sin. Today children are encouraged to understand that sin is a matter of making choices for which they are responsible, and to reconcile with those whom they may have offended.

SIN

Venial Sins. A venial sin is an act that is not fully consistent with an orientation toward God and Christian morality.

Mortal Sins. A sin is considered mortal if (1) the act was seriously sinful, (2) the sinner knew it was seriously sinful, but (3) did it willingly with full awareness that it was a rupture with God, the world, and the self.

An older man and his parish priest conduct confession in the pre–Vatican II style, in private, in the darkened confessional. At the end of their meeting the priest raises his hand to make the sign of the cross over the penitent, thereby absolving him of his wrongdoing. This kind of meeting has largely been replaced by face-to-face meetings in the light of day. A service for communal penance and general absolution has developed since Vatican II, though it is not often used.

Sin   Hell

THE SEVEN DEADLY SINS

1. Pride
2. Avarice
3. Lust
4. Anger
5. Gluttony
6. Envy
7. Sloth

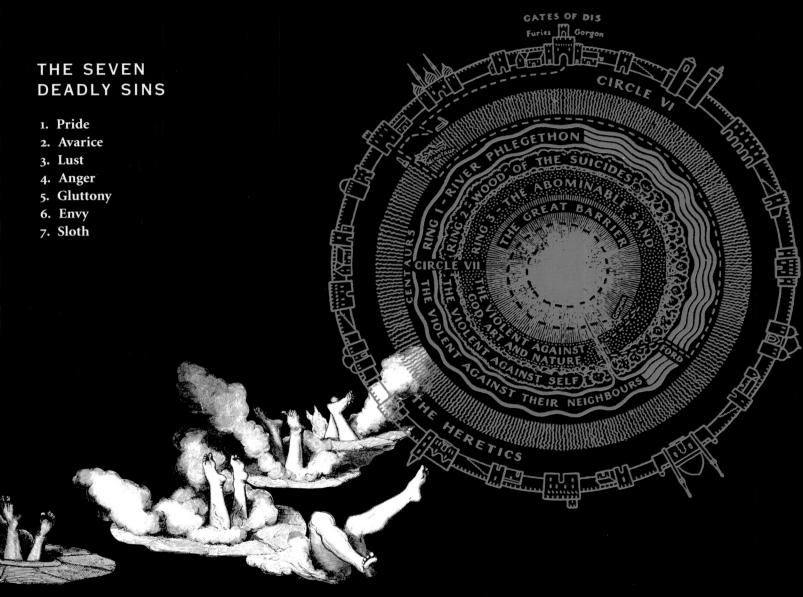

Hell. The literature of the underworld has attracted the talents of artists from ancient Egypt to Tibet. Few, however, can compare to the efforts of the medieval Catholics in Europe, who created hells more miserable and relentless than any that had come before. Dante Alighieri in the first book of his *Divine Comedy*, the *Inferno*, sketched out twenty-four descending circles of punishment and pain for sinners of all varieties. This drawing shows the scenery awaiting those guilty of violence. Today, Catholics define hell as "the eternal loss of God," and the Church has never positively affirmed that there is even one human being who is definitely in hell.

Heaven

Virtue

THE SEVEN VIRTUES

1. Faith
2. Hope
3. Love
4. Prudence
5. Fortitude
6. Temperance
7. Justice

Celestial Hierarchy. In heaven, as in the Vatican, there is an evident hierarchy. In the celestial hierarchy, the ranks are as follows:

1. seraphim, cherubim, thrones;
2. dominions, virtues, powers;
3. principalities, archangels, angels.

Heaven. Heaven is defined as the place where a human being, in both body and soul, experiences the direct intuitive knowledge of God or the Beatific Vision. It is said to be an actual though unique place, since the body, which occupies actual space, needs some "place" in which to exist. This heaven of both body and soul distinguishes the Catholic heaven from the Gnostic or Eastern notion of a heavenly bliss experienced by a disembodied soul.

SAYING THE ROSARY

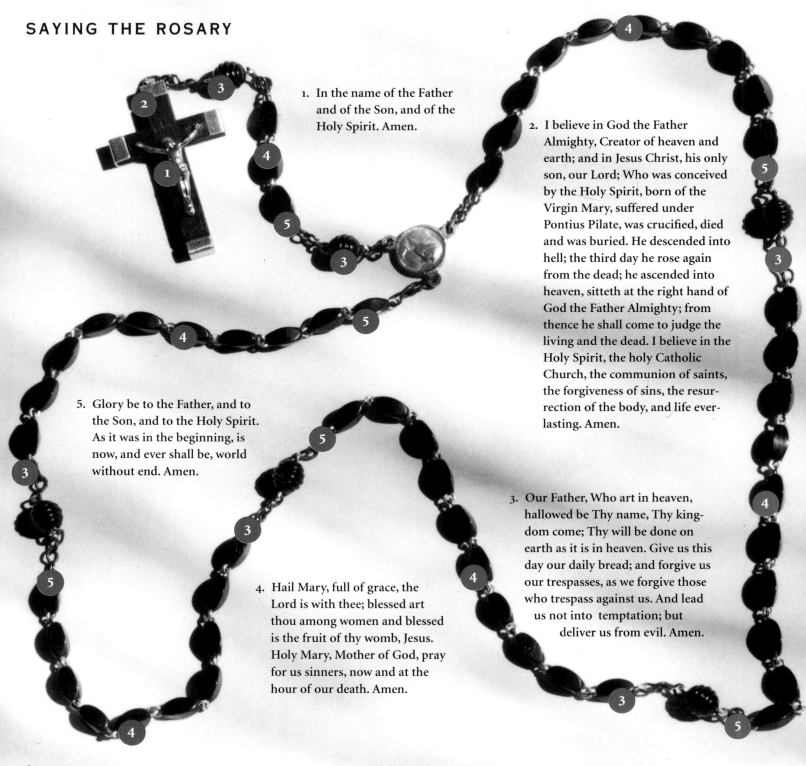

1. In the name of the Father and of the Son, and of the Holy Spirit. Amen.

2. I believe in God the Father Almighty, Creator of heaven and earth; and in Jesus Christ, his only son, our Lord; Who was conceived by the Holy Spirit, born of the Virgin Mary, suffered under Pontius Pilate, was crucified, died and was buried. He descended into hell; the third day he rose again from the dead; he ascended into heaven, sitteth at the right hand of God the Father Almighty; from thence he shall come to judge the living and the dead. I believe in the Holy Spirit, the holy Catholic Church, the communion of saints, the forgiveness of sins, the resurrection of the body, and life everlasting. Amen.

3. Our Father, Who art in heaven, hallowed be Thy name, Thy kingdom come; Thy will be done on earth as it is in heaven. Give us this day our daily bread; and forgive us our trespasses, as we forgive those who trespass against us. And lead us not into temptation; but deliver us from evil. Amen.

4. Hail Mary, full of grace, the Lord is with thee; blessed art thou among women and blessed is the fruit of thy womb, Jesus. Holy Mary, Mother of God, pray for us sinners, now and at the hour of our death. Amen.

5. Glory be to the Father, and to the Son, and to the Holy Spirit. As it was in the beginning, is now, and ever shall be, world without end. Amen.

Holy Rose is one of Mary's many names. From the Latin word *rosarium*, meaning "rose garden," we derive the name for the rosary. The prayers of the rosary are indeed like a garden of devotions centering around the Virgin Mary. Recitation of the rosary consists of fifteen decades of the Hail Mary, each introduced by the Our Father and concluded with the Doxology. Each set of ten Hail Marys is accompanied by meditation on one of the Mysteries, Joyful, Sorrowful, or Glorious, which refer to events in Christ's and Mary's lives.

MARY, QUEEN OF HEAVEN

Though excluded from the mostly masculine Holy Trinity (Father, Son, Holy Spirit), Mary's key role in Catholic worship has never faltered—a testament to the need for a feminine element in spiritual practice. In the fifteenth century, devotion to Mary was at its height. This painting combines the Immaculate Conception, the Assumption, and the Coronation of the Virgin. The instruments and sheet music of the heavenly choir are an accurate picture of medieval musical practice. Mary stands on a moon, another common symbol of the feminine presence.

Setting a standard that many mortal women have found difficult to emulate, Mary is celebrated in church literature for giving birth to Christ while still a virgin. She was not the first woman in history to give birth without male "intervention." Juno, the Roman queen of heaven, was said to give birth to her son Mars without sacrificing her virginity. Goddesses (and even gods) giving birth through means other than sexual union are common in ancient literature. Juno conceived Mars from the divine essence contained in a lily. In representations of the Virgin, Gabriel holds the lily, symbolizing Mary's acceptance of the life force through the flower. Both the lily and the rose are symbols of Mary.

THE VIRGIN OF GUADALUPE

In 1521, the Spanish conquered the empire of the Aztecs in what is now Mexico City. Ten years later, with Aztec culture in its death throes, Juan Diego, an Indian peasant, was walking by the hill that was the sacred abode of a version of their Mother Goddess. A woman appeared, and spoke to him in his native language Nahuatl: "Do not be afraid, you have nothing to fear, am I not here, your compassionate mother." The lady of this visitation became known as Our Lady of Guadalupe. In her image the aboriginal spirit of the universal Mother and the overlaid spirit of the Virgin Mary "Mother of God" are joined.

THE SACRED
CALENDAR

6

The sacraments and other rituals of the Church are rooted in an annual cycle of seasons and feasts with the celebration of Easter at its center. In one sense, every Sunday is a celebration of the Resurrection of Christ. Nevertheless, Easter occupies a unique place in the Church's sacred calendar. At the end of Lent is Holy Week, a time set aside for the preparation of the Easter celebration. The core of Holy Week is the Easter Triduum—Holy Thursday, Good Friday, and Holy Saturday—and its climax, the Easter Vigil, when new members are initiated into the Church, and then Easter Sunday itself. The importance of Easter is reflected in the fifty days that the season continues from Easter Sunday to Pentecost Sunday, when the Church recalls the sending of the Holy Spirit and the commissioning of the apostles to preach and teach to all nations.

The Resurrection of Christ on Easter is preceded by the penitential season of Lent, a forty-day period of prayer and fasting which begins with Ash Wednesday. Here a priest anoints parishioners with ashes, while saying the words, "Remember now that you are dust, and to dust you shall return." The ashes used for Ash Wednesday are set on a stone symbolizing the earth to which all shall return.

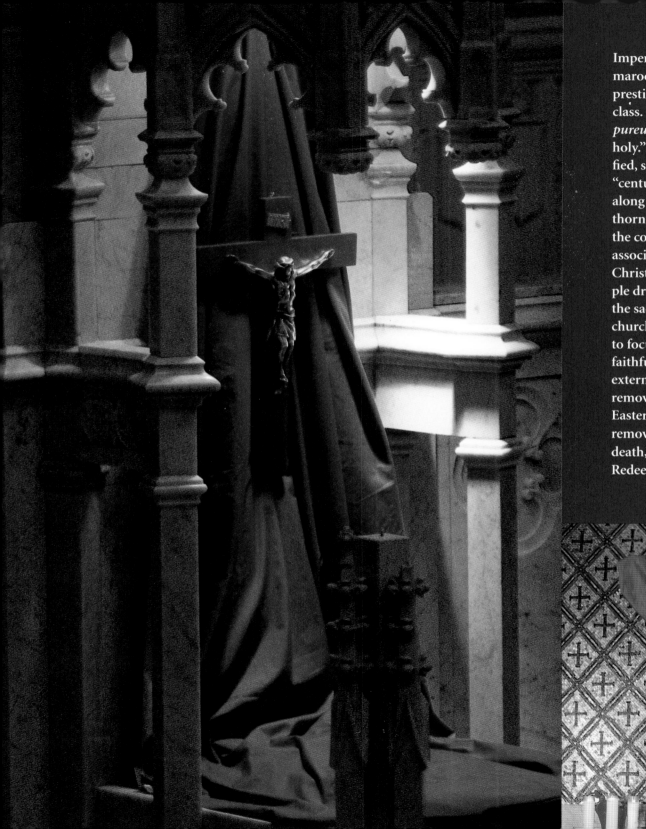

Imperial purple (almost maroon) was the color of prestige for the Roman ruling class. The Latin word *purpureus* actually means "very holy." Before Christ was crucified, soldiers draped him in a "centurion's purple cloak," along with the crown of thorns to mock him; and so the color purple came to be associated with the Passion of Christ. Now during Lent, purple drapery is used to cover the sacred images in some churches, a practice designed to focus the attention of the faithful inward, away from external images. The dramatic removal of the drapery on Easter also reflects the removal of the darkness of death, which Christ as Redeemer brought to all.

Palm Sunday. Palm fronds line the aisle of a church on Palm Sunday, the Sunday before Easter. The Romans used palm fronds as symbols of victory, waving them as they returned from victorious battles. When Jesus entered Jerusalem the week before his death, crowds that had gathered for Passover greeted him on the road with palm fronds crying out, "Hosanna, blessed is the King of Israel who cometh in the name of the Lord." Since then Christ's approaching victory over death, through the Resurrection on Easter, is prefigured in the palm. Each household takes a palm leaf home to remind it of Christ's triumph. The following year, old palms are returned to the church where they are burned. These ashes are used to anoint foreheads on Ash Wednesday. Thus the palm as a symbol of everlasting life is transformed into a symbol of mortality, then again renewed.

PALM SUNDAY

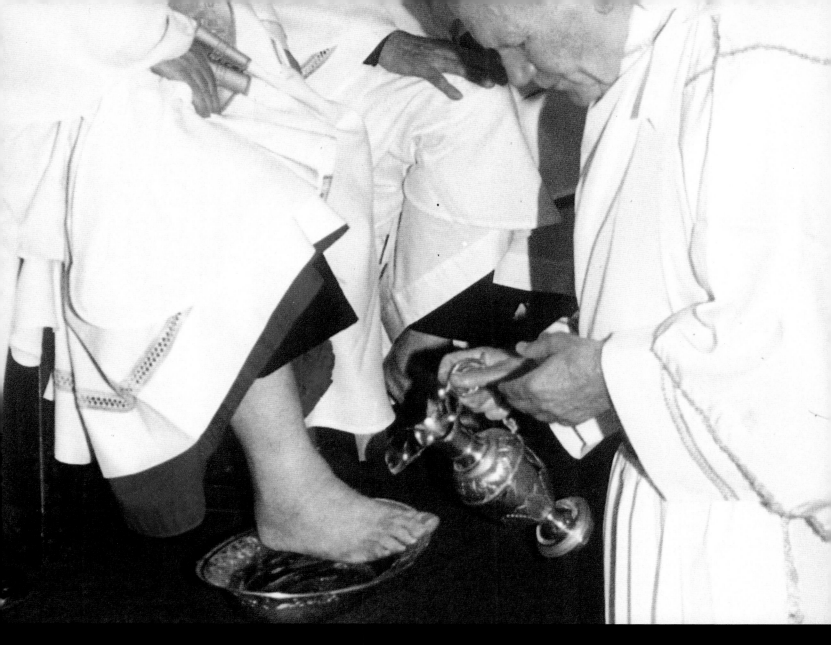

HOLY THURSDAY

Pope John Paul II washes the feet of his bishops on Holy Thursday. Before the Last Supper, Christ washed the feet of his disciples as an example of the humility and service he wished them to share with others. Footwashing was commonly done by slaves in the households of Christ's time, but has continued as a ceremony marking the beginning of the Easter Triduum since the thirteenth century.

STATIONS OF THE CROSS

This traditional Catholic devotional practice has its origins at least as early as the fourth-century pilgrimages to the holy sites associated with Christ's suffering and death in Jerusalem. By the twelfth century the Crusades and a heightened devotion to the Passion of Christ created a heavy demand in Europe for some pictorial representations of the main events toward the end of Jesus' life. In the beginning, however, there was no set number of "stations," or stopping-off points for meditation and prayer, on Jesus' final journey from Pilate's court to Calvary. The current number of fourteen first appeared in the Low Countries in the sixteenth century and was later made standard by various papal decrees in the eighteenth century. There is a custom of singing a stanza of the medieval hymn *Stabat Mater* ("By the Cross her station keeping") between each station. Modern liturgists insist that there should be a fifteenth station, namely, the Resurrection, which is the triumphant completion and fulfillment of the Passion and death of Jesus.

1. *Jesus is condemned to death.* Pontius Pilate, the Roman official, sentences Jesus to death and the angry crowd refuses his offer to release Jesus (Matthew 27:11–26).

2. *Jesus takes up his cross.* After the Roman soldiers mocked him and spat upon him, they gave him a cross to carry and led him away to Calvary (Matthew 27:27–31; Luke 23:26; John 19:17).

3. *Jesus falls the first time.* None of the three falls is recorded in the New Testament, but are assumed, by tradition, to have occurred.

4. *Jesus meets his mother.* Again, there is nothing in the New Testament to indicate that Jesus met his mother along the way to Calvary, unless she was among the women of Jerusalem, whom he did meet (Luke 23:27–29).

5. *Simon of Cyrene helps Jesus carry his cross.* Simon, "a passer-by, who was coming in from the country," was compelled to assist Jesus in carrying the cross (Mark 15:21; Luke 23:26).

6. *Veronica wipes the face of Jesus.* There is no mention of Veronica in the New Testament account of the way of the cross. The incident is a matter of pious tradition.

7. *Jesus falls a second time.*

8. *Jesus meets the women of Jerusalem.* Jesus tells the grieving women not to weep for him but rather for themselves and for their children, because the day of judgment is coming (Luke 23:28–29).

9. *Jesus falls a third time.*

10. *Jesus is stripped of his garments.* The New Testament does not mention this explicitly, but it is logical that the soldiers would have done so before nailing him to the cross.

11. *Jesus is nailed to the cross.* It is a traditional belief that Jesus was actually nailed to the cross, although none of the four New Testament accounts actually says that.

12. *Jesus dies on the cross.* While enduring his final suffering, Jesus spoke to the good thief who was crucified with him, with his mother and the apostle John, and to his Father in heaven (Matthew 27:44,45–46; Mark 15:34; Luke 23:43,46; John 19:25–27,30).

13. *Jesus is taken down from the cross.* The body of Jesus was given over to Joseph of Arimathea, a disciple of Jesus and "a respected member of the council" (Mark 15:43–46).

14. *Jesus is placed in the tomb.* Joseph of Arimathea laid the body in a new tomb "hewn out of rock" and then "rolled a stone against the door of the tomb" (Mark 15:46).

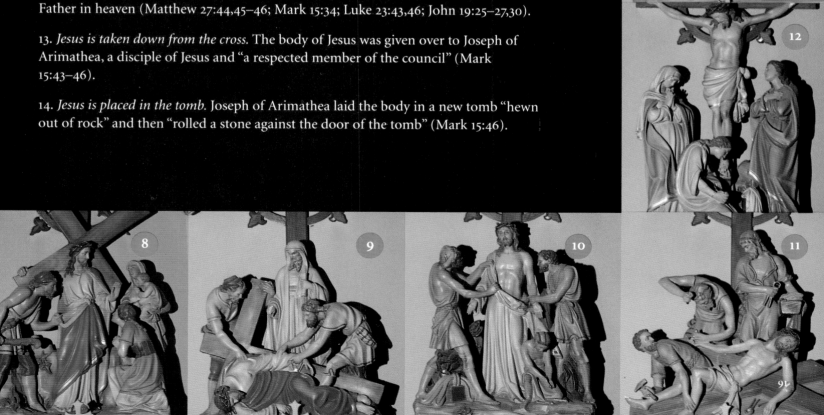

The Easter Passion in Guatemala. In Antigua, Guatemala,
Holy Week, or *Semana Santos,* is celebrated with high
drama. Hundreds of faithful dress in the clothing of
Romans and Israelites, some as soldiers, others as
mourners, recreating the scenes of Christ's crucifixion.
The processions move along elaborate carpets, or
alfombras, made of flower petals and sawdust, which are
destroyed by the passing procession only to be recreated
for the next day.

Roman soldiers placed a crown of thorns on Christ's head to mock the name given to him by his followers—Jesus of Nazareth, King of the Jews.

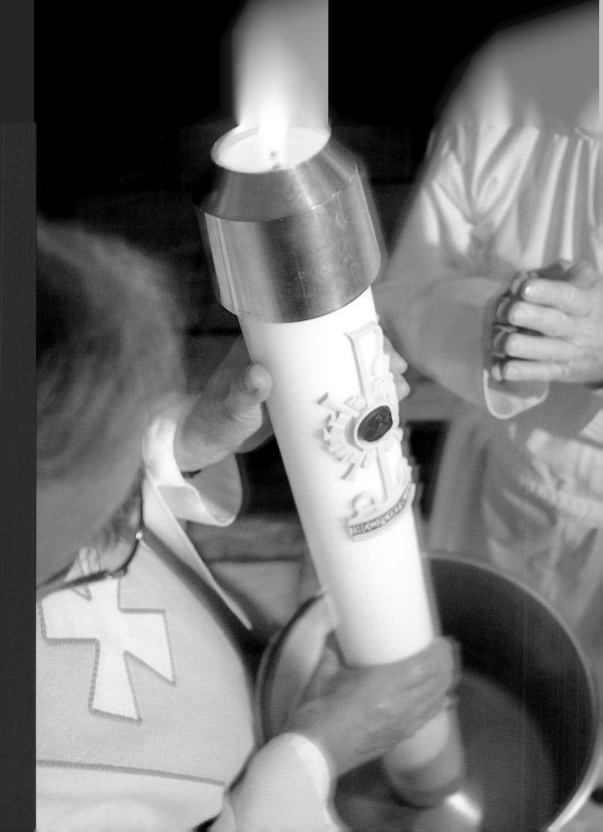

The Easter Vigil service originally lasted throughout the night as a true vigil kept in expectation of Christ's Resurrection on Easter morning. It is at this solemn Mass that new initiates are baptized into the Church. It is also the time when the paschal fire, representing Christ's Resurrection as "the light of the world," is kindled. From the fire, the Paschal Candle is lit and all other candles in the church are lit from this single candle, which is lit anew each year. Before baptizing the new catechumens, the newly lit Paschal Candle, representing the Body of Christ, is plunged into the font of baptismal water to bless the water with Christ's presence. Since some version of a springtime fertility ritual was practiced by almost all premodern cultures, and in world mythology water is primarily a female element and fire male, it is likely that this ritual has origins in much older rites. It would be an appropriate reference to the Easter season of birth and renewal through the new life that Jesus brings.

EASTER SUNDAY

The feast of Easter is celebrated on the first Sunday after the first full moon after the spring equinox. As the natural world bursts forth in the bright light of spring, Catholics celebrate the risen Christ, who brings them new life, in this existence and beyond.

The lily is an ancient symbol of spring. Like the lotus, the lily was seen as a cup that held the divine essence of life. It was an emblem of the springtime goddess Eostre, from which the word Easter derives.

At the other end of the year is the feast of the Nativity. Christmas is second only to Easter in its sacred importance. Like Easter, Christmas is preceded by a four-week-long season of joyful expectancy and hope known as Advent, for the coming of Christ's arrival — not only his coming on Christmas, but at history's end as well. The Christmas cycle runs from Christmas Eve to the Sunday after the Epiphany, or after January 6 if Epiphany is celebrated on Sunday. Apart from the Easter and Christmas cycles, the rest of the liturgical year is composed of thirty-three (or -four) neutral weeks known as Ordinary Time. The last Sunday on the Church's sacred calendar is the Solemnity of Christ the King, which anticipates the fulfillment of all of time, when Christ will restore all things to God. Throughout the year many individual feast days commemorate the anniversaries of the saints and martyrs, and especially the Blessed Virgin.

The Advent Wreath. The season of Advent is marked in Catholic homes and churches with the Advent wreath. One candle is lit each Sunday leading up to Christmas, until all four are illuminated, heralding the arrival of Jesus Christ, "the Light of the World." Violet candles are often used, with one pink candle for the third Sunday of Advent. Known as Gaudete Sunday, this festive Mass begins, *Gaudete in Domino semper*, "Rejoice in the Lord always."

"Up in the heavens a star gleamed out, more brilliant than all the rest; no words could describe its lustre, and the strangeness of it left men bewildered. The other stars, the sun and moon gathered round it in chorus, but this star outshone them all. Great was the ensuing perplexity; where could this newcomer have come from, so unlike its fellows? Everywhere magic crumbled away before it; the spells of sorcery were all broken, and superstition received its death blow. The age-old empire of evil was overthrown, for God was now appearing in human form to bring in a new order, even life without end."

From Ignatius's letter to the Ephesians, early second century AD

The Nativity. In the thirteenth century, St. Francis of Assisi began celebrating Christmas in a barn with animals and straw. Since then, Nativity sets, or scenes, have come to represent the miraculous events surrounding Jesus' birth. Here a priest blesses the church crèche on Christmas morning.

The Christmas Altar. Before Christianity, the Christmas season was celebrated in Europe as the feast of the Yule—a time to rekin-dle the light of the darkened sun, as it began to burn bright again after the winter solstice (around December 21). Evergreens, lighted trees, and gift giving all stem from the Yule feast, adopted like many traditions into the stream of Christianity.

Feast of the Assumption.
Celebrated on August 15, the feast of the Assumption celebrates the miraculous entrance of Mary's physical body into heaven. The story, of fourth-century origins, goes that several apostles who were present at Mary's death went away for a short time and returned to find her tomb empty. In this painting by Poussin a flock of *putti* sprinkle flower petals in the empty tomb, while Mary is escorted into the clouds.

St. Jacques Day. Some missionaries cite the persistence of voodoo as one of the difficulties with the Church in Haiti, where West African beliefs have blended into the faith practiced by over six million Catholics. Here, an open air Mass is celebrated in honor of St. Jacques on July 26. St. Jacques is a *loa,* or deity, with an authoritarian and warlike character, who wields power and control in the arts of war and battle. He may be related to St. Joachim, the father of the Virgin Mary, whose day he shares and who, according to legend, was fabulously wealthy.

ILLUSTRATED GLOSSARY

Alb   The long white tunic that is worn under the priest's chasuble, and worn by deacons and others assisting in the Mass. It is meant to resemble the white gown put on after Baptism and to remind the wearer of his or her own vows as a Christian.

Altar   The table on which the Eucharist is celebrated. Its origin is in the Old Testament where God commanded Moses to build "an altar of earth" on which to present "burnt offerings" and "offerings of well-being" (Exodus 20:24). As a symbol of Christ, who is the true sacrifice, altars are accorded a special reverence: the priest kisses the altar at the beginning of Mass; it is incensed during Mass; and it is reverenced with a deep bow when one passes in front of it during a ceremony.

Ashes   The residue of palms that are burnt on Passion Sunday (also known as Palm Sunday), ashes signify penance and reconciliation. The Catholic usage can be traced back to the Jewish custom of sprinkling ashes on the head as a sign of repentance. They are presently used on Ash Wednesday, when applied to the forehead, and in the rite for the dedication of a church.

Chalice   The cup used for wine and the Precious Blood at Mass. At the Last Supper Jesus "took a cup, and after giving thanks he gave it to [his disciples], and all of them drank from it. He said to them, 'This is my blood of the covenant, which is poured out for many'" (Mark 14:23–24). The chalice is also a symbol, therefore, of the sacrifice that Christ endured for the salvation of humanity and of the sacrifices that would be expected of his disciples (Mark 10:38).

Chasuble   The outer liturgical vestment worn by the priest at Mass. It is derived from a large cone-shaped, cloth garment called a *casula* (Latin, "little house") worn in the ancient world of Greece and Rome. By tradition the chasuble is a symbol of charity.

Chrism oil   The oil of olives mixed with perfume that is blessed by the bishop every year at the Chrism Mass, usually held on Holy Thursday morning. Chrism oil is used for anointing in the sacraments of Baptism, Confirmation, and Holy Orders, and for the dedication of churches and altars. Another kind of holy oil is used in the sacrament of the Anointing of the Sick.

Crosier   The crook-shaped staff, similar to that of a shepherd, used by bishops during ceremonies and in processions. Although its original significance is unknown, it is generally regarded as a symbol of the bishop's pastoral or shepherding office.

Genuflection   The flexing of one's right leg, with the knee touching the ground, as a sign of reverence before the sacramental presence of Christ. This gesture is made as one enters and leaves a church where the Blessed Sacrament is reserved in the tabernacle.

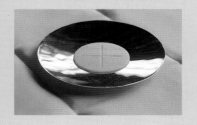

Host   The eucharistic bread. Derived from the Latin *hostia*, "victim," the word recalls Christ as the Paschal Lamb who was sacrificed for the salvation of all humanity. The consecrated host sits on a **paten,** a small, circular, flat dish (Latin, *patena*). Originally made of glass, it is now gold-plated metal. The paten and the chalice rest on the **corporal,** a square piece of linen.

Incense   The aromatic gums of resinous trees that are burned upon charcoal in a thurible. Incense is used in processions and to reverence sacred objects: the altar, the Gospel book, the Blessed Sacrament, and members of the worshiping congregation, including the clergy, religious, and laity.

Monstrance   A vessel used to display the host for public viewing. It is made of precious metal and is usually in the shape of a cross or a rising sun. A central flat window, or lunette, encases the host. Its use was derived from an earlier reliquary glass cylinder which was used to display the entire body, or body parts, of martyrs.

Palms   Blessed and distributed on Palm Sunday (the Sunday before Easter), palms are considered a sacramental of the Church, that is, a source of grace expressive of the faith of those who use them for devotional purposes. Palms are carried in procession to commemorate Christ's triumphant entry into Jerusalem shortly before his death. The Palm Sunday observance has its origin at least as early as the fourth century.

Presidential chair   The seat from which the priest who presides at Mass leads the congregation in prayer when he is not at the altar itself. The presidential chair is always situated in a place of prominence, usually in front of the altar, facing the people.

Rosary   A popular form of devotion to the Blessed Virgin Mary, the rosary, although attributed to St. Dominic, achieved its present form in the sixteenth century. The term derives from the Latin *rosarium*, "rose garden," which came to mean a collection of devotional texts. It consists today of fifteen decades of Hail Marys, each introduced by the Our Father and ended with the Doxology—each counted on a string of beads. For many in the Middle Ages, it served as a replacement for the Psalter, containing 150 psalms.

Sanctuary   The space in a church that immediately surrounds the altar. It is also called the chancel or choir. Before the Second Vatican Council (1962–65), it was separated from the congregation by an altar rail.

Stole   A narrow strip of fabric worn over both shoulders (by bishops and priests) or over the left shoulder (by deacons). Traditionally, the stole was worn under the chasuble, but today it is usually worn outside and over the chasuble.

Tabernacle   A niche or cupboard used to store the hosts for the Eucharist. It has a door that locks with a key, and is placed in a prominent location in the church. In modern churches it usually has a chapel or area of its own. In older churches it is behind the high altar. Hosts stored here are usually reserved for Communion for the dying or adoration in the monstrance.

GENERAL GLOSSARY TERMS

Ascension   The bodily translation of the risen Christ from earth to heaven (Luke 24:50–51; Acts 1:2–12). It signifies his vindication over his enemies as well as his enthronement at the right hand of God (Acts 2:33–36; Hebrews 1:3–4). The event is commemorated in the feast of the Ascension, which is observed on the Thursday before the seventh Sunday of Easter (roughly forty days after Easter), and which is a holy day of obligation in the Catholic Church. This means that all Catholics are bound to attend Mass on that day.

Assumption   The bodily translation of the Blessed Virgin Mary from earth to heaven. Although not attested to in the Bible, the dogma of the Assumption was solemnly proclaimed by Pope Pius XII in 1950 and the event is celebrated in the feast of the Assumption on August 15, which is a holy day of obligation in the Catholic Church. This means that all Catholics are bound to attend Mass on that day.

Catechumen   An unbaptized person who is undergoing instruction and spiritual formation in preparation for entrance into the Church. The catechumen is distinguished from those who are already baptized in another church but who are seeking full communion with the Catholic Church. These are called candidates. The process by which a catechumen is prepared for entrance into the Church is called the Rite of Christian Initiation of Adults (RCIA). It reaches its culmination at the Easter Vigil when the catechumen receives the three sacraments of initiation: Baptism, Confirmation, and Eucharist.

Gospel   The old English word means "good news." Gospel is the proclamation of the good news of salvation in Jesus Christ (Mark 1:1). The word *gospel* also refers to the four books of the New Testament attributed to Matthew, Mark, Luke, and John. The first three are called "synoptic," because their many parallels become evident when the texts are viewed together. The last is often referred to simply as "the Fourth Gospel."

Laity   Derived from the Greek word meaning "people." Laity are the Christian faithful, including clergy and religious. Over time, however, the term came to be limited to nonclergy and nonreligious, and that is still its popular meaning. The Second Vatican Council (1962–65) played a major role in restoring the importance of the laity, with its emphasis on Baptism, lay ministry, coresponsibility in the Church, and the vocation to transform the world.

Liturgy   Derived from the Greek word meaning "work of the public." Liturgy is the public and official worship which the Church gives to God in union with Jesus Christ and through the power of the Holy Spirit. Liturgy applies in the first instance to the Eucharist, or Mass, but also to all of the sacraments and to the Divine Office as well. The purpose of liturgy is the glorification of God and the sanctification of humanity.

Mission of the Church   Derived from the Latin verb *mittere*, "to send." Mission refers to that for which the Church has been "sent" by Christ into the world: "Go therefore and make disciples of all nations . . ." (Matthew 28:19). The mission of the Church includes at least four functions: proclamation of the word, celebration of the sacraments, service to those in need, and witness to the truth of the Gospel by the example of the Church's own life.

Mysticism   The intense and immediate experience of the presence of God, and of a deep communion of love and knowledge with God as well as with other people and all of reality. There are two common types of Christian mysticism: the way of stillness, of imagelessness, and of wordlessness (known as the apophatic approach); and the way of imaging God through words and the imagination (known as the kataphatic approach).

Sacraments   Seven sacred rituals officially sanctioned by the Church as signs and causes of grace. They include Baptism, Confirmation, Eucharist, Reconciliation (Penance, Confession), Marriage (matrimony), Holy Orders, and Anointing of the Sick (formerly, Extreme Unction). The real "last sacrament" is Viaticum, or final Communion.

Sin   Literally, a falling from the mark, that is, a failure to maintain in one's behavior and thought the standards of the Gospel of love, mercy, justice, forgiveness, and so forth. There are different kinds of sin. Original Sin is the condition into which all human beings are born because of the sin of the first parents, Adam and Eve. Actual sin is a specific violation of the moral order. Habitual sin is the sinful state that results from many actual sins. Another distinction is between mortal and venial sin; the former breaks the bond of friendship with God, while the latter weakens the bond. Theologians today add a third category, known as serious sin, that falls between mortal and venial.

Trinity   The doctrine that there are three Divine Persons in the one God: the Father, who is the Creator; the Son, who is the Redeemer; and the Holy Spirit, who is the Sanctifier. This is the central mystery of Christian faith because it reveals that God at once transcends us (the Father) and has been intimately present to us in the flesh (the Son), and that God remains with us as a force for healing, renewal, reconciliation, and communion (the Holy Spirit).

Vatican   An independent state in Italy governed by the earthly head of the Catholic Church, namely, the Bishop of Rome, also known as the pope. The Vatican is usually taken to be identical with the whole administrative bureaucracy of the Church: pope, Roman Curia, and Vatican City State together. It became a separate political entity in 1929 with the signing of the Lateran Treaty between the pope and the Italian government.

Vatican II   The twenty-first ecumenical council of the Catholic Church, held between 1962 and 1965. It was the largest (over 2,600 bishops attended), most representative (bishops from all over the globe), and most ecumenical council in history, with every major Christian church represented by official observers. A reformist council called by Pope John XXIII (d. 1963), it emphasized the role of the laity in the Church and the role of the Church in the modern world.

SELECTED BIBLIOGRAPHY

Flannery, Austin, O. P., ed. *Vatican Council II: The Conciliar and Post Conciliar Documents.* Vatican Collection, Vol. 1. Northport, New York: Costello Publishing Company, 1992.

Flinders, Carol Lee. *Enduring Grace: Living Portraits of Seven Women Mystics.* San Francisco: Harper Collins, 1993.

Johnson, Kevin Orlin. *Expressions of the Catholic Faith: A Guide to the Teachings and Practices of the Catholic Church.* New York: Ballantine Books, 1994.

McBrien, Richard. *Catholicism,* Rev. ed. San Francisco: Harper Collins, 1994.

————, ed. *HarperCollins Encyclopedia of Catholicism.* San Francisco: Harper Collins, 1995.

Metford, J. C. J. *Dictionary of Christian Lore and Legend.* London: Thames and Hudson, 1985.

Merton, Thomas. *The Seven Storey Mountain.* New York: Harcourt, Brace, Jovanovich, 1948.

O'Shea, Father Bill. *Questions Catholics Ask.* San Francisco: Harper Collins, 1990

Pennington, Basil M. *Praying by Hand, Rediscovering the Rosary as a Way of Prayer,* Rev. ed. San Francisco: Harper Collins, 1995.

Pope John Paul II and Cardinal Bernard Law, frwrd. *The Pope Speaks to the American Church.* San Francisco: Harper Collins, 1992.

Walsh, Michael. *Dictionary of Catholic Devotions.* San Francisco: Harper Collins. 1993.

————, ed. *Butler's Lives of the Saints.* Tunbridge Wells, Kent, England: Burns & Oates, 1985.

ACKNOWLEDGMENTS/PHOTO CREDITS

The editors would like to thank the following people who graciously shared with us their Catholic faith and practice. In San Francisco: Mt. Rev. John Raphael Quinn, Archbishop of San Francisco; Mt. Rev. Carlos A. Sevilla, Bishop of San Francisco; Rev. Msgr. John J. O'Connor and the parish of Mission Dolores Church; Rev. Charles R. Gagan and Rev. Jim Fletcher of St. Ignatius Church; Rev. Michael J. Healy and the children of St. Philip the Apostle School; Kathy Carey and Rev. Thomas S. Merson of Saint Mary's Cathedral; Rev. John F. Baldovin of the Jesuit School of Theology in Berkeley; Tony LaTorre at Old Saint Mary's Church; Elaine Lancelotti and the students of St. Patrick's Church in Larkspur; Rev. Edward J. Ludeman; Rev. Mark V. Taheny; Rev. Thomas Hayes of Most Holy Redeemer Church; Angel at St. Paul of the Shipwreck Church; Rev. Msgr. Fred A.L. Bitanga of St. Patrick's Church; Robert Mesko; Randall Lyman; Wendy and Michael Roman; Michael Temperio; Elizabeth Walker; Scott and Josef Nygaard; Lisa and David Robles; and Dashiell MacNamara. In Lincoln, Nebraska: Mt. Rev. Fabian W. Bruskewitz, Bishop of Lincoln; Msgr. Ivan F. Vap of the Cathedral of the Risen Christ; Albert and Eleanor Hamersky and family; Rev. Kenneth Borowiak, Church of the Assumption in Dwight; Rev. Edwin Stander of Sacred Heart Church; Sr. Barbara Ann Braun, St. Elizabeth's Hospital; Kevin Weiland and family; Lupe Opp and family; Rev. Daniel J. Seiker; Gilbert Novacek; John Osmera; Ted Milburn; Bill Knight; Chad Greenway; Ed and Jana Parr; Andy McCarville; and Ryan Sweeney.

All photos are by © 1995 Anne Hamersky except for the following.
Page 14, 15, 18, 19, 20: © 1995 Gianni Giansanti/SYGMA; 21: © 1995 Franco Origlia/SYGMA; 23: Perugino, *The Crucifixion with the Virgin, Saint John, Saint Jerome, and Saint Mary Magdalene* (left panel), Andrew W. Mellon Collection, © 1995 Board of Trustees, National Gallery of Art, Washington; 28: Workshop of Albert Altdorfer, *The Fall of Man* (middle panel), Samuel H. Kress Collection, © 1995 National Gallery of Art, Washington; 30: Raphael, *The Alba Madonna*, Andrew W. Mellon Collection, © 1995 Board of Trustees, National Gallery of Art, Washington; 36: © 1995 Stephanie Compoint/SYGMA; 62: © 1995 Nicholas Devore III/ Photographers Aspen; 69: © 1995 Gianni Giansanti/SYGMA; 78: Drawings by C. W. Scott-Giles courtesy Penguin Ltd. and Gustave Doré; 79: Drawing by Gustave Doré; 81: Master of the St. Lucy Legend, *Mary, Queen of Heaven*, Samuel H. Kress Collection, © 1995 Board of Trustees, National Gallery of Art, Washington; 89: © 1995 Alberto Pizzoli/ SYGMA; 92, 93: © 1995 E. Pasquier/ SYGMA; 102: Nicholas Poussin, *The Assumption of the Virgin*, Ailsa Mellon Bruce Fund, © 1995 Board of Trustees, National Gallery of Art, Washington; 103: © 1995 Lynne Warburg/Swanstock.